ADVENTURES WITH ROCKS AND MINERALS

BOOK *II*

GEOLOGY EXPERIMENTS FOR YOUNG PEOPLE

—Adventures with Science—

Lloyd H. Barrow

ENSLOW PUBLISHERS, INC.

44 Fadem Road	P.O. Box 38
Box 699	Aldershot
Springfield, N.J. 07081	Hants GU12 6BP
U.S.A.	U.K.

DEDICATION
To members of my family—Rosemary, Len, and Valerie

ACKNOWLEDGMENTS
I wish to thank Mark Miles and Shai Ingli for typing,
Don Pershar for the graham cracker activities, and teachers
and graduate students for their comments and suggestions
during the preparation of this book.

Library of Congress Cataloging-in-Publication Data

Barrow, Lloyd H.
    Adventures with rocks and minerals. Book II : geology
experiments for young people / Lloyd H. Barrow.
      p. cm. — (Adventures with science)
    Includes index.
    ISBN 0-89490-624-0
    1. Geology—Experiments—Juvenile literature. I. Title.
II. Series.
QE44.B37 1995
550'.78—dc20
                                       94-29234
                                            CIP
                                           AC

Printed in the United States of America

10 9 8 7 6 5 4 3 2 1

Illustrated by Kimberly Austin Daly

CONTENTS

INTRODUCTION

GEOLOGY

Right under our feet, the earth is changing. Rocks are forming from molten materials deep down in the interior of the earth. Continents are moving. Mountains are rising and then slowly wearing away.

People who study the earth and how it changes are called geologists. They learn about the earth by making observations, by asking questions, and then by experimenting to find the answers. Some of the questions geologists ask are easy to answer. To find out if a diamond can scratch glass, a geologist just gets a diamond and some glass and observes what happens when the diamond is rubbed against the glass. But some of the questions are trickier, such as "How old is the earth?" and "How do mountains form?"

As geologists find answers to their questions, they always come up with new questions and experiments. My first book, *Adventures with Rocks and Minerals: Geology Experiments for Young People*, contained thirty experiments and suggestions for additional activities. This book is a collection of another thirty experiments about geology that you can do at home or in school. Doing them will help you learn how to ask questions and find answers and how to become a better observer. No one will ever know everything about geology—but it's great fun to learn as much as you can about it.

THE EARTH

Geologists believe that the earth is over 4.5 billion years old. When it first formed, it was so hot that it was molten—liquid rock. Over the ages, the outside layer of the earth, called the crust, has slowly turned solid, but most of the inside is still molten. As continents form and move over millions of years, pressures deep inside the earth cause earthquakes and volcanoes. As layers of rock push against one another,

4

moved by these forces inside the earth, sometimes they fold over one another the way a stack of washcloths folds up if you push on both ends. This folding is one of the ways mountains form. Another way mountains form is when the pressure inside the earth splits a layer of rock. The split is called a fault. Once mountains form, wind and rain slowly wear them away in a process called weathering. These changes take place over thousands or even millions of years, so people can't observe them firsthand. But geologists can observe how things are today and read about how things were a hundred years ago from earlier scientists who wrote down their observations. Then they can make educated guesses (hypotheses) about how things came to be this way and how they might change in the future. Geologists can never be absolutely certain that their hypotheses are right, but experiments help them to learn if they are on the right track.

Rocks are made up of minerals—crystals of different chemicals. Each mineral has its own special properties. In order to identify a mineral, geologists observe its color and shape and experiment to discover its other properties.

Geologists classify rocks into three types, based on the three ways that rocks form. (1) Igneous rocks form from molten rock that hardens as it cools down. Lava from volcanoes turns into igneous rock. (2) As rocks are worn away by moving water or wind, they are sometimes ground into sand or silt. Sedimentary rock forms when this sand or silt is pressed and cemented together. Sandstone is an example of a sedimentary rock. (3) If an igneous or sedimentary rock is heated and compressed by forces in the earth so much that its minerals are changed, it forms a metamorphic rock. Marble is a metamorphic rock.

Soil is formed by the breaking down of rocks by weathering and by the actions of living things. This process takes such a long time that when soil is carried away by the wind or rain, which is called erosion, it may not be replaced for thousands of years. Consequently, soil is very valuable, which is why geologists study it and help farmers to conserve it.

Geologists also study earthquakes. The more they learn about them from the past, and the more observations they make about present earthquakes, the better they can prepare us for future ones.

ADVENTURES WITH GEOLOGY

This book is a collection of questions and experiments to help you understand how a geologist studies the earth. Each experiment has five parts. The <u>materials</u> part lists what you need. The <u>procedure</u> explains how to do the experiment safely. The <u>observations</u> suggest some of the things to look for. The <u>discussion</u> explains what your observations may tell you about geology. The <u>other things to try</u> part suggests more questions and gives you hints about how to discover more about geology.

SAFETY NOTE

WHEN YOU DO THESE EXPERIMENTS MAKE SURE YOU

1. Get an adult's permission before using anything in your home.
2. Ask an adult to watch you do the experiment. Grownups are interested in the earth, too!
3. Carefully follow the directions for each experiment.
4. Clean up when you're finished.
5. Have fun!

HOW ARE SEDIMENTARY ROCKS FORMED?

Materials
Ruler
Hammer
Wax paper
Scissors (kitchen)
Small tomato paste can, with its top and bottom lids removed
Ten Gummi Bears™ of each color—red, green, yellow, and orange
Dowel rod about one inch in diameter and at least two inches
    longer than the can

Procedure
Set the can upright, with its top and bottom lids removed, on a flat surface. Place one lid from the tomato paste can inside the can so that it is flat against the bottom. Cut a piece of wax paper so that it lines the inside of the tomato paste can, and sticks out of the top. Using the kitchen scissors, cut the red Gummi Bears™ into small pieces and put them in the can. Then do the same with the green, yellow, and orange Gummi Bears™. Be sure to clean the scissors thoroughly to remove the stickiness. These pieces of Gummi Bears™ represent sediments (pieces of minerals). Place the other lid on top of the last layer of Gummi Bears™. Gently set the dowel rod on top of the lid. Measure the length from the bottom of the can to the top of the dowel rod. WITH AN ADULT'S HELP, carefully hit the top of the dowel 20 times with the hammer. Now measure the length from the bottom of the can to the top of the dowel rod again.

To remove the Gummi Bears™, turn the can upside down and tap gently. The wax paper and lids should prevent them from sticking to the can. Remove the wax paper and examine the layers of different colors.

Observations

How are the squeezed Gummi Bears™ different from the layers of cut Gummi Bears™? How many colored layers are there? Which layer is the thickest? How did squeezing the Gummi Bears™ affect the height of the rod? How difficult is it to separate the layers?

Discussion

This experiment is a model of how sedimentary rocks are formed,

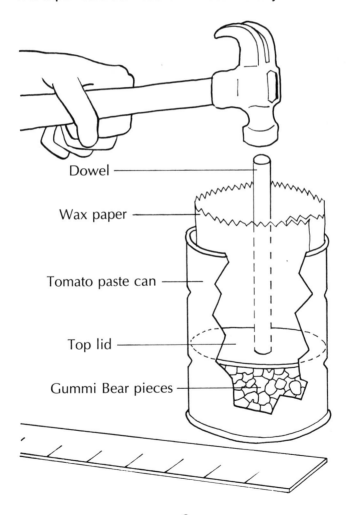

Dowel

Wax paper

Tomato paste can

Top lid

Gummi Bear pieces

although Gummi Bears™ will never become hard enough to form rocks.

Sedimentary rocks are formed when sediments are squeezed together. This squeezing leaves less space between the sediments. The weight of deposits of more sediments on top causes this squeezing. Squeezing the Gummi Bears™ by hitting the dowel with the hammer acted like the weight of other deposits. Minerals, such as calcite, quartz, and hematite, "glue" the sediments together. The sugar in the Gummi Bears™ glued the cut up pieces together.

Sedimentary rocks are deposited in layers. Geologists know that the oldest layer is always on the bottom and the youngest is on the top. So, your red Gummy Bear™ layer is the oldest and your orange layer is the youngest. It is easier to separate these layers than to break across them. Another common feature of sedimentary rocks is that they may contain the fossils of animals and plants that lived when the rocks were formed.

Other things to try

Examine the layers of common sedimentary rocks such as limestone, sandstone, shale, and coal, and compare their thicknesses.

Repeat the experiment, hitting the dowel 30 times to see how much further the Gummi Bears™ can be compressed.

Examine sedimentary rocks in your backyard or around your school for various fossils.

With an adult, go to a sedimentary rock quarry or to a roadcut (a road or highway that goes through layers of rock) and study the various layers of rock.

Take pieces of shale and other sedimentary rocks and put them in water, then smell them. Compare the earthy smell of shale with that from other sedimentary rocks.

HOW ARE IGNEOUS ROCKS FORMED? **2**

Materials
Sauce pan
Wax paper
Hand lens or magnifying glass
Aluminum pie tin which fits inside sauce pan
Five Gummi Bears™ of each color—red, green, yellow, and orange

Procedure
HAVE AN ADULT HELP YOU WITH THIS EXPERIMENT! Place the sauce pan on the burner on your stove. Set an aluminum pie tin in the bottom of the pan. Place all the Gummi Bears™ in the pie tin. Turn the burner on to medium. Do NOT cover the pan. Do NOT look down into the pan because it could splatter in your face. When most of the Gummi Bears™ have melted, turn off the burner. Leave the pan on the burner for ten minutes to cool. Remove the pan from the burner and let it stand overnight.

The next day, remove the aluminum pie tin from the pan and turn it upside down onto the wax paper. Tap the bottom of the tin to get the melted Gummi Bears™ out. Using the hand lens, examine both the Gummi Bears™ that melted and the ones that did not.

Observations
How are the melted Gummi Bears™ different from the unmelted Gummi Bears™? How did the colors change? Did crystals form on the melted Gummi Bears™? What do they look like?

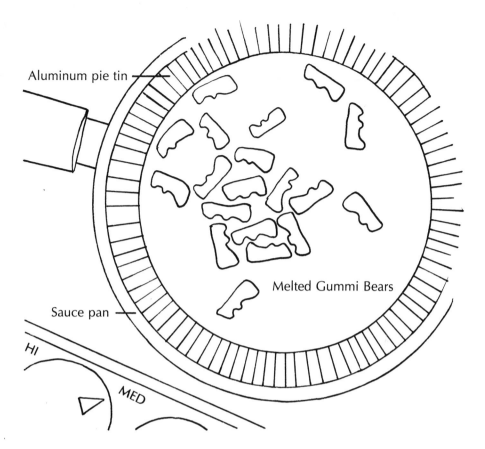

Aluminum pie tin

Melted Gummi Bears

Sauce pan

HI

MED

Discussion

This experiment is a model of how igneous rocks are formed. Geologists describe any rock that has been melted as igneous. Igneous rocks are formed when melted rocks cool.

Geologists believe that the core of the earth is very hot. Even though geologists have not dug into the core, they have noticed temperatures become higher the deeper they drill. Sometimes, hot material from the core, in the form of melted rock, comes all the way to the surface and forms volcanoes. Frequently, however, this melted rock does not reach the surface and begins to cool very slowly. As it cools, mineral crystals grow and become large. When melted rocks come to the surface, they cool rapidly and their mineral crystals are smaller. For example, granite is formed inside the earth and is a coarse-grained igneous rock. Basalt is cooled at the surface and is a fine-grained igneous rock. Obsidian comes from volcanoes and is cooled so quickly that crystals do not have time to form.

Other things to try

Repeat the experiment, but let all of the Gummi Bears™ melt. This time, after you turn off the burner, let the pan cool for ten minutes. Have an adult remove the aluminum pie tin and place it in ice water. Compare the crystal size.

Using a hand lens, compare the crystal sizes of granite and basalt.

Using a hand lens, examine the glossy appearance of a piece of obsidian. Notice its sharp edges. In prehistoric times, obsidian was used for items such as spearheads and knives.

HOW ARE METAMORPHIC ROCKS FORMED?

Materials

Ruler
Hammer
Wax paper
Scissors (kitchen)
Ten Gummi Bears™ of each color—red, green, yellow, and orange
Small tomato paste can, with its top and bottom lids removed
Dowel rod about one inch in diameter and at least two inches
   longer than the can

Procedure

Set the can upright, with its top and bottom lids removed, on a flat surface. Place one lid from the tomato paste can inside the can so that it is flat against the bottom. Cut a piece of wax paper so that it lines the inside of the tomato paste can, and sticks out of the top. Using the kitchen scissors, cut the red Gummi Bears™ into small pieces and put them in the can. Then do the same with the green, yellow, and orange Gummi Bears™. Be sure to clean the scissors thoroughly to remove the stickiness. These pieces of Gummi Bears™ represent sediments (pieces of minerals). Place the other lid on top of the last layer of Gummi Bears™. Gently set the dowel rod on top of the lid. Measure the length from the bottom of the can to the top of the dowel rod. WITH AN ADULT'S HELP, carefully hit the top of the dowel 20 times with the hammer. Now measure the length from the bottom of the can to the top of the dowel rod again. This represents a sedimentary rock. Carefully hit the top of the dowel rod an additional 50 times with the hammer.

To remove the Gummi Bears™, turn the can upside down and tap gently. The wax paper and lids should prevent them from sticking to the can. Remove the wax paper and look at the layers of different colors.

Observations

Now how many colored layers are there? Which layer is the thickest? How did hitting the Gummi Bears™ affect the height of the rod? How difficult is it to separate the layers? How have the pieces of Gummi Bears™ changed?

Discussion

This experiment is a model of how metamorphic rocks are formed. Metamorphic rocks are formed when already existing rocks are

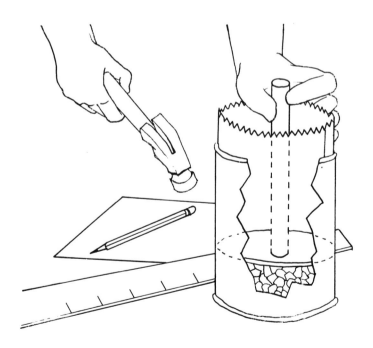

changed by heat, pressure, and/or chemical reaction without melting. "Meta" means change. Hitting the dowel rod increased the pressure on the Gummi Bear™ pieces. The pressure and resulting heat almost melts the pieces, making them denser. Metamorphic rocks frequently have bands that resemble layers. These rocks are reformed in many different ways. For example, geologists know that limestone becomes the metamorphic rock marble, shale becomes slate, and sandstone becomes quartzite.

Other things to try

Examine pieces of common metamorphic rock such as marble, shale, and quartzite with a hand lens.

Examine equal sized pieces of marble and limestone. Compare their weights.

Compare the weights of the same sized pieces of slate and shale.

Wet pieces of shale and slate and compare their odors.

WHAT HOLDS SANDSTONE TOGETHER? 4

Materials

Salt	Teaspoon
Fine sand	Newspaper
Ruler	Pencil/pen
Two Styrofoam cups	Hand lens or magnifying glass
Paring knife	Ferrous sulfate iron tablets (available at
Tablespoon	drug stores)

Procedure

With your ruler, measure about 1.5 inches (2.7 cm) from the bottom of the two Styrofoam cups. Draw lines around the cups at this height. Using the paring knife, carefully cut the cups at the line. Label one cup "salt" and the other cup "iron." Put about 1 inch (2.5 cm) of water in each cup. To the cup marked "salt," add one-fourth teaspoon of salt and stir until the salt dissolves. To the cup marked "iron," add five crushed ferrous sulfate iron tablets. To crush the tablets, put one tablet in a tablespoon. Set a teaspoon on top of the tablespoon and with your fingers push the two spoons together, crushing the iron tablet. Crush the other four iron tablets separately. Sprinkle the crushed iron tablets on the water in the cup and stir until the tablets dissolve. Slowly sprinkle fine sand (not sandbox sand) into both cups until the sand becomes wet and almost reaches the top of the cup.

Set the cups in a place where they will not be moved. After five days, the water will probably evaporate. Spread three or more layers of newspaper on a flat surface. Carefully cut the sides of the Styrofoam cups away and gently remove the sand. Examine the sand with your hand lens or magnifying glass.

Salt, water, and
sand mixture

Iron, water, and
sand mixture

Observations

In which containers were the sand particles held together? Which were the easiest to break apart? What color was the material holding the sand together?

Discussion

In this experiment, the iron made a piece of sandstone, a sedimentary rock. Geologists have studied what cements (joins together) individual pieces of sand. Ferrous sulfate is a common cementing material in forming sandstone. Geologists have noted that some types of sandstone break apart easier than others. This is because there was less cementing material in the water when that sandstone was formed. Frequently, the reddish or yellowish coloring of sandstone is due to the dissolved iron (ferrous sulfate) in the water.

Other things to try

Repeat the experiment with other powders such as sugar and epsom salt.

Repeat the experiment with iron tablets other than ferrous sulfate.

WHAT HAPPENS WHEN YOU RUB ROCKS TOGETHER? 5

Materials
Shoe box with lid
Magnet
White paper
Old nylon stocking
Hand lens or magnifying glass
Sandstone pieces (available from rock shop)

Procedure

Take two pieces of sandstone that are different colors. Sandstone is an example of a sedimentary rock. Examine each piece with the hand lens. Notice the color, size, and shape of the various sand grains/minerals. Touch the magnet to each piece. If it sticks, there are magnetic materials in the sandstone.

Spread out a few pieces of paper on a large surface. Rub the two pieces of sandstone together fifty times. Be careful not to hit your fingers. As you rub them together, pieces should come off. Push the pieces together in one pile. Place the magnet in the pile. Check to see if any pieces stick to the magnet. Remove any of these pieces from the magnet and return them to the pile. Sift the pieces of sand through an old nylon stocking over an empty shoe box. Put what remains in the stockings into the lid of the shoe box. Examine each group with your hand lens.

Observations

What different colors were found in the sandstone? What was the shape of the corner of the pieces of sand? What was the color of any that were magnetic? How does rubbing change the edges of the pieces? In which pile did you have the most pieces—those that went through the openings of the stockings or those that did not?

Discussion

Sandstone is a sedimentary rock with loosely-connected minerals. When you rub sandstone rocks together, pieces of sand come off. Because there are spaces between the pieces of sand in sandstone, it is ideal for water to pass through.

Some grains are different sizes and colors. Geologists have noticed that specific minerals such as magnetite are sometimes found in sand. The pieces that stick to your magnet are probably magnetite. The clear, shiny pieces are probably mineral quartz. Rounded corners

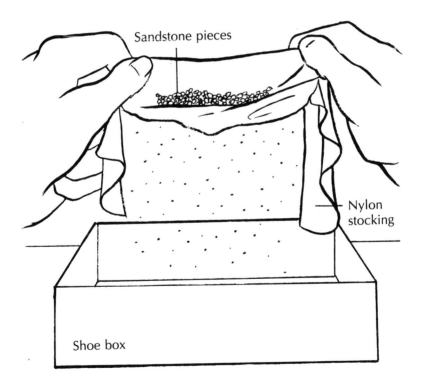

Sandstone pieces

Nylon stocking

Shoe box

indicate to geologists that the sand grains have been carried a distance which caused the sharp edges to be broken off.

Machines grind up sandstone to be used for sandpaper. Large pieces of sand that did not go through the stockings could be used to make coarse sandpaper. The pieces that went through the stockings are smaller and could be used in making fine sandpaper.

Other things to try

Repeat the experiment with two pieces of the same colored sandstone. Compare the amount that goes through and stays inside the nylon.

Make sandpaper by gluing sand onto heavy paper and letting it dry for several days.

Compare the number and size of sand grains on coarse and fine sandpaper in an area the size of a quarter.

HOW MANY LAYERS ARE THERE IN COAL?

Materials
Ruler
Needles
Modeling clay
Piece of wood larger than the piece of coal
Hand lens or magnifying glass
Piece of coal (either from rock shop or coal company)

Procedure

With a ruler, measure the thickness of the piece of coal. Coal is made up of layers of dead plants that have been hardened into rock. Coal is an example of a sedimentary rock. With your hand lens, count the number of layers and notice how thick they are.

Flatten the clay onto the wood. Gently press the flat surface of the coal into the clay. The clay will hold the coal in place while you are working on it.

To separate the layers of coal, carefully insert a few needles underneath the top layer. Push the needles in until the top layer becomes loose. You may want to ask an adult to help you in prying the layers apart. Examine the bottom of the top layer and the top of the second layer with your hand lens.

Sometimes, you will find a twig or leaf impression preserved in the coal. This is a fossil (remains of a once-living plant or animal that has been preserved in the rock). Continue separating the layers of coal and examine each layer.

Observations

How many layers are there in your coal? Which are the thickest and thinnest layers? If you found a fossil, what does it look like?

Discussion

Coal is an example of a sedimentary rock. Coal is formed when plants die and fall into a body of water. They sink to the bottom and

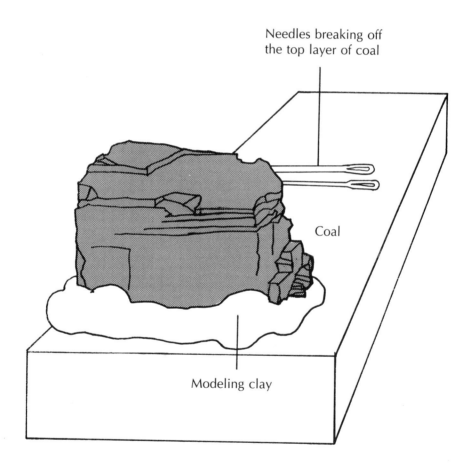

Needles breaking off
the top layer of coal

Coal

Modeling clay

pile up. Then, they are rapidly buried by thick layers of sediments in the water. The weight of the sediments makes them flat and squeezes out the water, making thin layers. Over time, the water dries up, leaving sediments hardened into layers of rocks and coal. During mining, the coal is separated from the rock.

Not all dead plants and animals become fossils. To become a fossil, a dead plant or animal must become buried very rapidly to prevent it from decaying. Generally, only hard parts such as shells, teeth, and bones become fossils.

Geologists believe that coal areas were swamps millions of years ago. There are two types of coal—bituminous (soft coal) and anthracite (hard coal). Layers of coal can be very thin (not worthy of mining) or very thick. Sometimes geologists have to dig deep in the earth to get coal. Coal is a nonrenewable resource. This means there is only so much that is available on the earth.

Coal is called a <u>fossil fuel</u>. It is made up of very old plant matter that can be burned to give off a large amount of heat. Although we can burn coal for heat, it gives off fumes that pollute the air. Because it pollutes, coal is rarely used for heating homes anymore. Instead it is more commonly used in manufacturing, like steel.

Other things to try

Compare equal-sized pieces of bituminous and anthracite coal to see which is heavier.

Repeat the experiment, comparing the difficulty of separating layers of bituminous and anthracite coal samples.

Turn a sample of coal on its edge and hit it with a hammer. Frequently, the layers will come apart. Check to see if fossils are present.

WHAT IS THE DIFFERENCE BETWEEN **7** A BOULDER, COBBLE, AND PEBBLE?

Materials
BBs
Scissors
Metric ruler
Pen
Mustard seed
Lid to 18-ounce jelly jar
10-inch dinner plate
Several pieces of corrugated cardboard

Procedure

ASK AN ADULT TO HELP YOU WITH THIS EXPERIMENT.

Lay a dinner plate face down on a piece of cardboard and trace around the edge. With scissors, cut out the circle. Any rock that will not fit through this opening is called a boulder. Lay a jelly jar lid on another piece of cardboard and trace around it. Cut out the circle. Rocks that will fit through the boulder opening but not through this opening are called cobbles. Lay a BB on a piece of cardboard and trace around it. Carefully cut out this small circle (measuring with the ruler, its diameter should be 4 mm). Rock pieces which fit through the cobble opening but not through this opening are called pebbles. Lay a mustard seed on another piece of cardboard and trace around it. Cut out this 2-mm circle. Any rock that goes through this opening is called soil. Lay the pieces of cardboard on top of one another, with the smallest opening on the bottom and the largest on top. Gather a pile of rocks and one at a time determine which are boulders, cobbles, pebbles, and soil.

Observations

Of which size rock did you find the most—boulders, cobbles, pebbles, or soil? Compare the colors of the rocks.

Discussion

Geologists use size to describe rocks or pieces of rock. They use the same sizes, whether the type of rock is igneous, metamorphic, or sedimentary. When rocks are weathered, they are broken into smaller pieces. So, boulders become cobbles, cobbles become pebbles, and pebbles become soil. Even soil is categorized by the size of its particles. The largest soil particle is sand, which can be weathered into silt which, in turn, can be weathered into clay. The following chart is used by geologists to categorize pieces of rock:

Term	Metric Particle size cm (mm)
Boulder	more than 25.6 (256)
Cobble	6.4-25.6 (64-256)
Pebble	0.4-6.4 (4-64)
Granule	0.2-0.4 (2-4)
Sand	0.006-0.2 (.06-2)
Silt and clay	<0.006 (<.06)

Geologists use wire screens, each with different sized openings (sieves), to measure the sizes of rocks. These are usually stacked on top of one another, just like your cardboard openings. The sieves on the top always have the largest opening and those on the bottom have the smallest opening.

Other things to try

Examine piles of rocks in your neighborhood. Determine what is the most common size.

Break a cobble to see how many pieces of pebbles are formed.

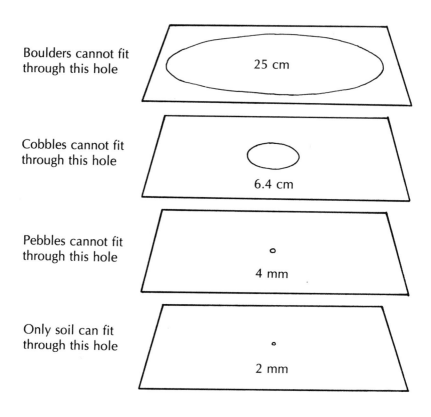

Boulders cannot fit through this hole — 25 cm

Cobbles cannot fit through this hole — 6.4 cm

Pebbles cannot fit through this hole — 4 mm

Only soil can fit through this hole — 2 mm

HOW CAN YOU DETERMINE THE TYPE OF SOIL?

Materials
Ruler
Teaspoon
Medicine dropper
Samples of soil

Procedure
Geologists use a simple test to determine whether a sample of soil contains mainly sand, silt, or clay. Measure about 2 teaspoons of soil, and place it in the palm of your hand. Using the medicine dropper, add water to the soil a drop at a time. Knead the soil until it is like a moist putty. If it is too wet, add dry soil and knead until it is easily molded into a ball. Place the ball of soil between your thumb and forefinger. Using your thumb, gently push the soil so you are squeezing it upward into a ribbon. If no ribbon forms, the soil is mainly sand. Form a ribbon of even thickness and width. Let the soil ribbon emerge and extend over your finger. The weight of the ribbon will cause it to break. As it begins to break, measure its length with a ruler. If the ribbon is less than 2 inches (5 cm) when it breaks, the soil is mainly silt. If the ribbon is about 2 inches (5 cm) or more when it breaks, the soil has a large amount of clay.

Repeat the test with soils from different locations.

Observations
How long was the soil ribbon when it broke? What does the wet soil feel like? How do the colors and textures of the soils compare?

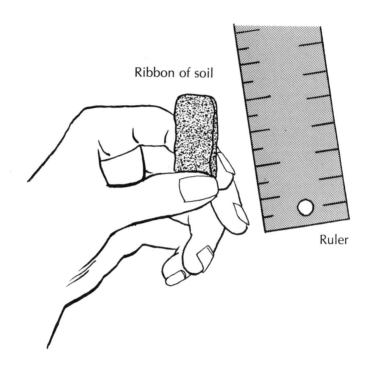

Ribbon of soil

Ruler

Discussion

Geologists identify sand as soil particles whose diameter is between 0.06 mm and 2.00 mm. Sand particles made into a ball do not hold enough water to make a ribbon. Geologists have also noticed that these coarse particles easily fall apart. Clay has the smallest soil particles, with diameters of less than 0.004 mm. Clay particles are able to hold a lot of water. This makes wet clay feel sticky and allows long ribbons to be formed. Silt particles are between the sizes of sand and clay (0.004 mm to 0.06 mm). When silt is made into a ball it holds some water and feels gritty (like flour). Because silt can hold some water, a short ribbon can be formed.

You can also figure out soil types after a heavy rain. A high area where water stands probably has a large quantity of clay and/or silt, while areas that drain rapidly have large amounts of sand. In dry months, sandy areas frequently will not have enough water between soil particles for plants to grow. An ideal soil would have about equal amounts of sand, silt, and clay.

Other things to try

Compare the type of particles found in topsoil (the dark layer of soil at the surface) and subsoil (the lighter layer of soil beneath the topsoil).

What happens to the soil ribbons when they dry out?

With an adult's permission, test the soil from a pot with plants in it.

If you visit friends and relatives who live in other places, test the type of soil where they live.

HOW CAN YOU DETERMINE ORGANIC MATERIAL IN SOIL? 9

Materials
Potting soil
Sand
Measuring spoons
Measuring cup
Tall thin jars with lids (such as an olive jar)
Several samples of soil
Powdered Alum (a spice available in grocery stores)

Procedure
Potting soil has a large amount of organic matter (dead plants) in it. To determine if organic matter is present, you will need to measure 1/4 cup (about 60 ml) of potting soil and put it in a jar. Add 1/2 teaspoon of powdered alum to the jar. Add 1 cup (about 250 ml) water to the jar. Tighten the lid and shake it vigorously ten times. Set the jar aside for one minute and then remove the lid. If there is organic matter present, material will be floating at the top.

Repeat the procedure using sand instead of potting soil. The lack of material floating at the top means that sand does not have organic matter. Test soil around your home to determine if it contains organic matter.

Observations
Of the soils you tested, which had about the same amount of organic matter as the potting soil? Does soil color indicate the presence of organic matter?

Discussion

In this experiment, you compared various soil samples for organic matter. Geologists have found that organic matter in soil varies from place to place. Generally, the darker the soil, the greater the amount of organic matter. The dark color is due to recently decayed plants and animals. More organic matter in soil results in better plant growth because the organic matter is a fertilizer. Organic matter is usually found only in topsoil (the dark layer of soil near the surface). The lighter colored layer below the topsoil is called subsoil. Potting soil is rich in organic matter. The dark brown-black soil has a loose, crumbly texture that allows space for air and water which can be used by growing plants.

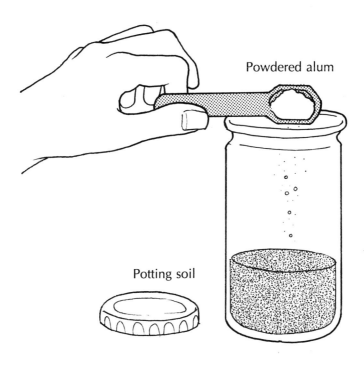

Powdered alum

Potting soil

When soil is low in organic matter, geologists recommend adding organic matter if the soil will be used for growing plants. Sometimes, farmers add organic matter by plowing green plants into the soil. Gardeners can add compost, manure, or peat moss before planting.

Other things to try

Test various samples of topsoil to see if one has more organic matter than another.

Are there more earthworms in soil with or without organic matter?

Compare plants grown in soils with high and low amounts of organic matter.

HOW DOES THE TYPE OF PLANT ROOT AFFECT EROSION?   **10**

Materials
Ruler
Trowel
Newspaper
Two jars you can put your hand inside
Hand lens or magnifying glass

Procedure

Erosion happens when wind or water carry soil away. This experiment will help you understand how plants affect erosion.

Ask an adult if you may dig up plants outside before beginning this experiment. Find a dandelion or a clump of dandelions. Using a trowel, dig up the entire dandelion plant. The root of a dandelion is a large, long, single structure that grows deep into the soil. Dig down in order to get as much of the root as possible. Lay the root and its soil on a newspaper.

Find an area of thick grass. Dig up a clump the same size as the diameter of a small glass. Dig until the roots are exposed. Lay the clump of grass and soil on another newspaper.

Hit the roots of each plant with the back of the trowel three or four times to remove loose soil. Now place the dandelion plant into a jar that is half-filled with water.

Place the grass in the other jar that is half-filled with water. Let each plant sit for one hour.

After one hour, reach into each jar and shake the plants in the water. Remove the plants and lay them on separate newspapers. Examine the dandelion roots with your hand lens. Remove one grass plant and examine its roots with a hand lens. With the ruler, measure the length of the roots.

Ask an adult where to dump the jars of water.

Dandelion and root

Grass and roots

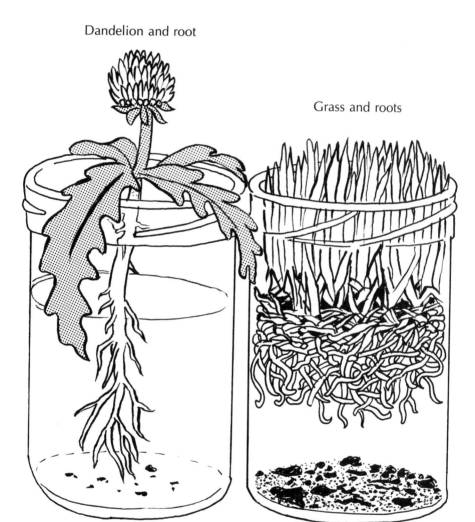

Jars half-filled
with water

Observations

Which jar had more soil in the bottom? Which plant had more roots? How long were the dandelion and the grass roots?

Discussion

Roots have special roles for plants. In addition to taking in water, they support the plant. Without a strong root system, wind could blow the plant away. But not all plants have the same type of root system. The dandelion is an example of a plant with a tap root (a single structure which is usually longer than your finger). A carrot is another plant with a tap root. Grass has a series of net roots (several inter-twined, thick, string-like roots). The net roots firmly hold the plant in place. That is why it is difficult to pull up grass. When you pull up tap root plants, usually little soil comes with the plant. However, net root plants have a lot of attached soil.

Geologists have noticed that fields with net root systems have less erosion. Grass plants that are very close together have roots growing in and among each other to form an interlocking system. Geologists recommend that plants with net type roots be planted on areas with steep slopes in order to reduce erosion. With a hand lens, you can see hair-like structures, called root hairs, coming out of the sides of roots. They help the plant get moisture. Because net root systems are shallow, they need more roots and root hairs to get water. A tap root grows downward rather than branching outward, leaving it without much to hold the soil in place. When a heavy rain or strong wind occurs, soil is carried away.

Other things to try

Compare various garden vegetables and flowers to determine their types of roots.

HOW DOES PLANTING UP AND DOWN THE SLOPE OF A HILL AFFECT SOIL EROSION?

Materials

Soil
Fork (Meat)
Water
Sprinkler can
Measuring cup
Masking tape
Two clear glasses
Two large shallow pans
Two half-gallon (two-quart) cardboard milk cartons
Four wood blocks (all same size) or bricks

Procedure

Cut away one side of each milk carton. With masking tape, tape the open spouts on the tops of the cartons shut. Using a measuring cup, fill the cartons with equal amounts of soil. It is best to fill them outside.

Stack two blocks, and prop one end of a carton on the blocks. The carton is now sloped like a hill. Do the same with the other carton using two more blocks. Place a large shallow pan under each of the cartons to collect the <u>runoff</u> (water not held by the soil). On one carton, start at the top of the hill and place a fork about 1 inch (2.5 cm) deep in the soil. Run the fork down the hill, making rows or furrows that go from the top to the bottom of the carton. Pour two cups (about 500 ml) of water into a sprinkler can, and gently pour it on the carton with the furrows. Refill the sprinkler can and pour the same amount on the

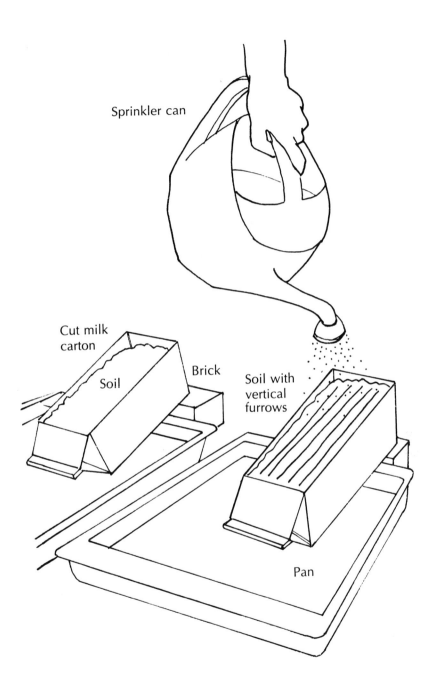

Sprinkler can

Cut milk
carton

Soil

Brick

Soil with
vertical
furrows

Pan

carton without furrows. Notice what happens to the furrows, soil, and water. When the water collects in the pans, measure how much water ran off each milk carton. Pour the water from the pans into two clear glasses and check to see which is cloudier.

Ask an adult where to dump the soil.

Observations

Which carton lost more soil (had more soil end up in the pan)? Which pan had cloudier water? How did the water affect the furrows? How do furrows running up and down a hill affect erosion?

Discussion

Rain can carry soils from one area to another. This process is called soil erosion. When farmers plant furrow crops (row crops) such as corn or beans up and down a hill, it causes more soil erosion because water tends to follow the vertical furrows. Planting around the hill (horizontal furrows) slows down the moving water. Geologists try to slow down fast-moving water by diverting it in several directions, blocking it with a dam, or planting trees or plants in the area. They may use a combination of these techniques. Because slow-moving water cannot carry as much soil, it deposits or drops it.

Other things to try

Repeat the experiment, using different heights (blocks).

Repeat the experiment, using cartons in which you have grown grass. In one carton, use the fork to make the same furrows or rows down the hill as you did before. Compare the results with those in which there was no grass.

HOW DOES PLANTING AROUND A HILL AFFECT SOIL EROSION?

Materials

Soil
Fork (Meat)
Water
Sprinkler can
Measuring cup
Masking tape
Two clear glasses
Two large shallow pans
Two half-gallon (two-quart) cardboard milk cartons
Four wood blocks (all same size) or bricks

Procedure

Cut away one side of each milk carton. With masking tape, tape the open spouts on the tops of the cartons shut. Using a measuring cup, fill the cartons with equal amounts of soil. It is best to fill them outside.

Stack two blocks, and prop one end of a carton on the blocks. The carton is now sloped like a hill. Do the same with the other carton using two more blocks. Place a large shallow pan under each of the cartons to collect the runoff (water not held by the soil). On one carton, place a fork about 1 inch (2.5 cm) deep in the soil and make several horizontal furrows running across (side to side, not top to bottom) the carton.

Pour two cups (about 500 ml) of water into the sprinkler can, and gently pour it on the carton with furrows. Refill the sprinkler can and pour the same amount on the carton without furrows. Notice what happens to the furrows, soil, and water. When the water collects in the pans, measure how much water ran off each milk carton. Pour the water into two clear glasses and check to see which is cloudier.

Ask an adult where to dump the soil.

Observations

Which carton lost more soil (had more soil end up in the pan)? Which pan had cloudier water? How did the water affect the furrows? How do furrows across a hill affect erosion?

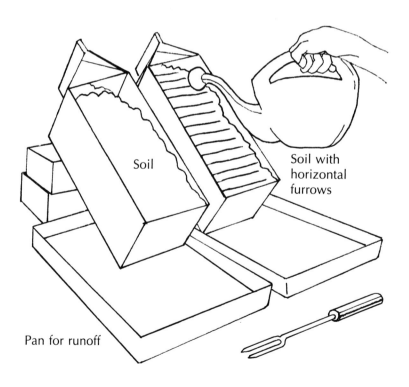

Soil

Soil with
horizontal
furrows

Pan for runoff

Discussion

Since rain is one cause of <u>soil erosion</u>, farmers plant furrow crops such as corn or beans in horizontal furrows. As you discovered in Experiment 11, planting around the hill in horizontal furrows slows down moving water, causing it to drop or deposit the soil it is carrying.

Other things to try

Repeat the experiment, using differing heights (more or less blocks). Repeat the experiment, using cartons in which you have grown grass. Make horizontal furrows in one. Compare the results with those in which there was no grass.

HOW DOES THE LAYER OF SOIL **13** AFFECT WATER HOLDING CAPACITY?

Materials

Bucket
Topsoil
Subsoil
Trowel
Two pans
Measuring cup
Masking tape
Rubber bands
Ruler
Pieces of old washcloths
Two 46-ounce juice cans, both ends removed

Procedure

Using a trowel, dig a hole straight down in the ground to a depth of at least 15 inches (40 cm). An adult will need to help you find a place to dig. Notice the different colors of the layers in the soil. If there is no color change, dig deeper. If there are no layers, you will need to dig in another location. The dark layer near the surface is called topsoil. The lighter color that is below the topsoil is called subsoil. Remove several cups of the darker topsoil and lighter subsoil for your experiment. Keep the different soils separate.

Wrap pieces of an old washcloth over one end of each of two empty juice cans. Hold the washcloths in place with rubber bands. Then tape the edges of the cloths around the cans. Place the juice cans in separate pans with the covered ends facing down. Slowly add 2 cups (about 500 ml) of topsoil to one juice can and 2 cups (about

500 ml) of subsoil to the other can. Gently shake the cans so the soil is at the same height. Slowly pour 1 cup (about 250 ml) of water into each juice can. After five minutes, carefully remove the cans and set them in a bucket. You will notice that some of the water remains in the pans. Measure and record how much water passed through the topsoil and through the subsoil into the pans. Pour the water and the soil in a place recommended by an adult.

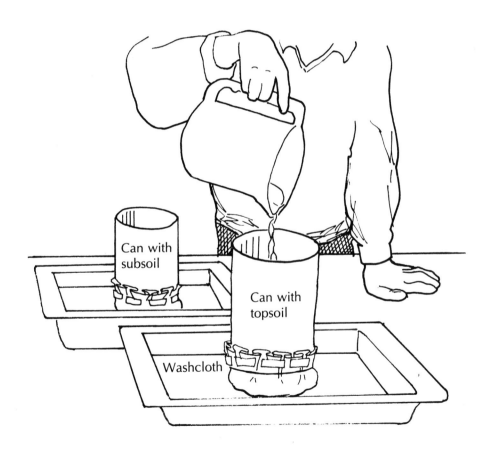

Observations

How much water went through the topsoil? How much water went through the subsoil? Which type of soil—topsoil or subsoil—had more water pass through it? How does the water look in the pans?

Discussion

The layer of soil where plants grow is topsoil. This dark brown or black layer has organic matter (dead plants or animals) that acts as a fertilizer, improving plant growth. Subsoil tends to lack organic matter. Crops do not grow as well in subsoil.

Water moves through different soils at different speeds. Geologists have noticed that the smaller the soil particles, the slower the water passes through the soil. Clay particles fit close together leaving little space for water movement. Geologists call the space between soil particles porosity. Generally, subsoil has lower porosity so water moves through it more slowly.

Other things to try

Repeat the experiment, using sand, potting soil, and clay. Compare the effects. How much water passes through in ten minutes? How much water passes through in one hour? What happens when you use a large amount of water?

How does hand packing the soil influence water movement, as compared to leaving the soil loose?

HOW DOES A WINDBREAK AFFECT SOIL EROSION?

14

Materials

Sand
Ruler
Bucket
Bricks
Potting soil
Small gravel
Large balloon
Measuring cup

Procedure

Mix together 1 cup (about 250 ml) each of potting soil, sand, and small gravel in a bucket. Pile the mixture on the ground about 3 feet (1 meter) from the side of a building. Blow up a balloon, holding the air inside with your fingers. Lay the balloon, still closed by your fingers, about 15 cm (6 inches) from the pile. The balloon will become your wind. Holding the balloon in place, let the air out while pointing it at the pile. Observe where the potting soil, sand, and gravel have been blown. Using the ruler, measure how far they have moved. Clean up the area when you have finished.

Prepare another identical mixture and pile it the same distance from the wall. Place bricks on edge in front of the pile. The bricks should be about double the length of the pile. Arrange the bricks so that any holes in them are not facing the pile. The bricks will become your windbreak, and will be used to stop the path of the wind. Blow up the balloon to the same size as before. Release the air from the

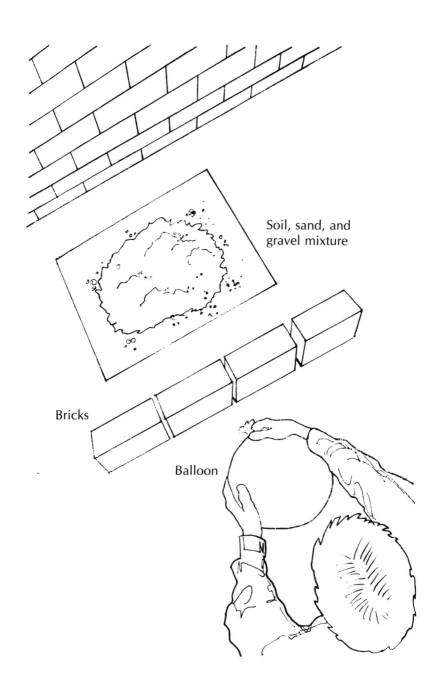

Soil, sand, and gravel mixture

Bricks

Balloon

balloon. Observe where the potting soil, sand, and gravel have been blown. Measure how far they have moved.

Clean up the area and dispose of the materials in a place specified by an adult.

Observations

Which material was blown the farthest by the wind, with and without the windbreak? Which were moved the least by the wind, with and without the windbreak? How do windbreaks affect soil erosion caused by wind?

Discussion

Winds are able to move large quantities of soil from one place to another. Geologists try to reduce wind erosion by blocking the path of the wind, which changes its direction and reduces its force. Farmers will frequently plant a row of trees to form a windbreak.

Geologists have noted that the lightest weight particles (potting soil) will be blown farther than heavier particles. Pieces of gravel will be moved the least. Strong winds are able to blow soil particles farther. Even with windbreaks, a strong wind can cause soil erosion.

Other things to try

Placing the balloon half the distance from the pile, repeat the experiment, with and without the bricks. What was the effect?

Look for evidence of soil erosion caused by wind in your neighborhood. Compare the amount of erosion to areas with windbreaks.

HOW DOES SOIL COMPACTION AFFECT WATER MOVEMENT IN SOIL?

15

Materials

Bucket
Measuring cup
Two pans
Masking tape
Rubber bands
Ruler
Potting soil
Pieces of old washcloths
Two 46-ounce juice cans, both ends removed

Procedure

Wrap pieces of an old washcloth over one end of each of two empty juice cans. Hold the washcloths in place with rubber bands. Then tape the edges of the cloths around the cans. Place the juice cans in separate pans with the covered ends facing down. Fill each of the cans completely to the top with potting soil. Gently shake the cans so the soil is at the same height. While one can sits in the pan, hand pack the soil by pressing down on it with your fingers several times. Check to make sure that the washcloth, rubber band and tape are still in place. Slowly pour 1 cup (about 250 ml) of water into each juice can. After five minutes, carefully remove the cans and set them in a bucket. Measure and record how much water passed through the packed and unpacked soil into the pans. Pour the water and the soil in a place recommended by an adult.

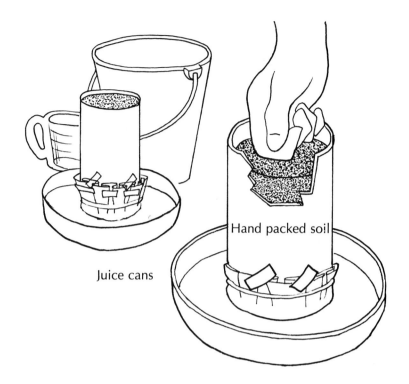

Juice cans

Hand packed soil

Observations

How much water passed through the unpacked potting soil? How much water passed through the packed potting soil? How does packing affect the amount of water that passes through soil? Compare the color of the water in the two pans.

Discussion

The space between the soil particles contains air that is used by soil animals such as earthworms. Rain goes into these spaces. Geologists have found that when there is less air space between soil particles, water tends to move through more slowly. When you hand packed one can, you were reducing the amount of air space in the soil. After a storm, compacted areas frequently have puddles of water.

A heavily traveled dirt walking path will be more compacted than the dirt a few feet off to the side of the path.

Other things to try

Repeat the experiment using sand.

Repeat the experiment by packing ten, and then fifty times by hand. Compare the amount of water that passes through the soil.

With the help of an adult, use a Phillips screwdriver and a hammer to compare the number of hits it takes to force the screwdriver into the compacted soil of a walking path and into the uncompacted soil about 3 feet (1 meter) off the path.

WHAT HAPPENS IN QUICKSAND?   **16**

Materials
Fine sand
Plastic straw
Scissors
Bucket
Ruler
Masking tape (or modeling clay)
Rock (about the size of your fist)
Large clear plastic jar

Procedure

Cut a small hole in the side of a large clear plastic jar. The hole should be about 1 inch (2.5 cm) above the bottom. Plug up the hole with masking tape or modeling clay so that water will not drain out. Fill the jar about half-full with fine sand, making sure the hole is plugged at the bottom. Very gently pour water down the inside of the jar until the water level is at the top of the sand. Looking through the side of the jar will help you determine how much water to add. Sprinkle a handful of sand onto the top. If it sinks into the water, continue adding handfuls of sand until all the water is covered. Lay a small rock on top of the sand. Let it sit for at least one minute or longer. If it sinks, remove the rock and add more sand. Then replace the rock. Set the jar in the center of a table. With your fist, hit the table near where the jar is sitting until the rock moves.

Remove the small rock. Add sand or water so that the water in the jar is up to the top of sand. Cut a plastic straw so it will lay across the sand without touching the sides of the jar. Hit the table near where the jar is and notice what happens to the straw.

Dump the sand and water in a place recommended by an adult. Rinse the jar several times to remove all of the sand.

Observations

What happened to the rock? How far did it sink into the sand? After hitting the table, how were the sand and water arranged? What happened to the straw?

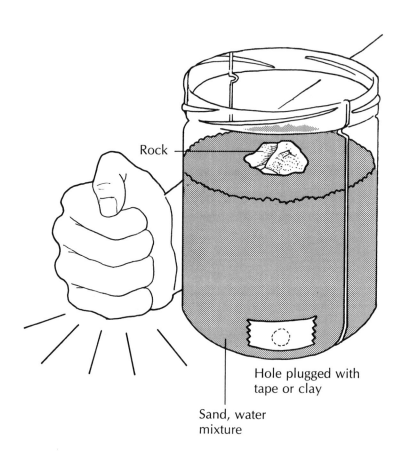

Rock

Hole plugged with tape or clay

Sand, water mixture

Discussion

Quicksand is an area of sand that when shaken acts like a liquid rather than a solid. Piles of sand have a large amount of air space between the particles. When water replaces the air, the sand can become quicksand.

In loose, dry sand, the weight of the top sand layers is supported by lower layers of sand. When water replaces the air space, the upper layers of sand are resting on the layer of water rather than on sand. A sudden shake, such as an earthquake, causes the entire area of wet sand to behave like thick liquid jello. As a result, heavy objects on top of the sand may sink. Only heavy objects sink into quicksand because wet sand is able to support light objects such as the straw.

Not all areas of sand can become quicksand. In quicksand, all the sand particles are about the same size and shape. So when you step on the soupy quicksand, the sand particles slide under your feet. Generally, quicksand is only about knee-deep. So, it is not usually dangerous, but it is messy and hard to get out of. Geologists have found that quicksand only occurs when there is a supply of water near the area of sand. When it becomes drier, quicksand loses its "liquid" properties.

Other things to try

Repeat the experiment using various objects to see if they sink in quicksand.

17

HOW DID GLACIERS AFFECT THE LANDSCAPE?

Materials
Sand
Small gravel
Bucket
Measuring cup
Brick
Sheetrock or smooth board (one to two feet in length)
Large, shallow pan
Half-gallon (two-quart) non-plastic milk carton
Hand lens or magnifying glass

Procedure
Put 1 cup (about 250 ml) of sand and 1 cup of gravel into an empty milk carton. Add water until it is almost full. Close up the flap and lay the carton on its side in a pan with the opening facing up. Put it into a freezer and leave it overnight.

Prop a piece of sheetrock on a brick to form a slight incline. Remove the milk carton from the freezer and peel the milk carton away from the frozen block. This block will be your glacier. Lay the roughest edge of the glacier at the top of the incline. Notice what happens as gravity very slowly pulls the glacier down the incline. Using the hand lens, check the path of the glacier on the sheetrock. When it reaches the bottom, place the glacier in a bucket.

Ask an adult to tell you where to dump your melting glacier.

Observations

How does the bottom of the glacier feel? How long does it take gravity to pull the glacier down the incline? Examine the path taken by the glacier with your hand lens. Gently rub your fingers down the path, and then up the path and compare.

Discussion

A glacier is a huge mass of compacted snow which becomes ice. As a glacier moves, it picks up soil and rocks. Glaciers are very large, and their weight causes them to flow down hills. This movement is very slow. As they move, the roughness at the bottom scratches rocks and other surfaces.

As glaciers slide down the side of mountains, geologists have noticed that they carve U-shaped valleys, in contrast to the V-shaped

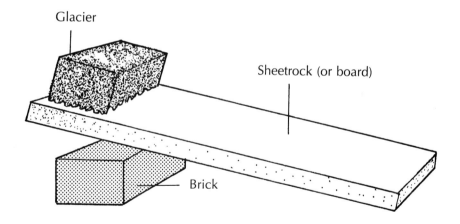

Glacier

Sheetrock (or board)

Brick

valleys made by rivers. If you visit the mountains, look for U-shaped valleys, a clue that they were formed by glaciers.

As a glacier melts, the soil and rocks inside are carried away by the moving water. Geologists have noticed that small pieces are carried farther than large pieces. The more a glacier melts, the farther pieces are carried.

Other things to try

Repeat the experiment using a quart-sized milk carton and 1/2 cup (125 ml) each of sand and gravel. Determine how weight affects the path marks.

Repeat the experiment with the sand and gravel at the bottom of the milk carton.

After the glacier has melted for 15 minutes, rub your hand up and down the bottom surface. Examine the embedded sand and gravel with a hand lens.

HOW IS A RIVERBED FORMED? **18**

Materials
Ruler
Sand
Measuring cup
Scissors
Brick
Large pan (or wading pool)
Sprinkler can
2-liter soda bottle
1/2-gallon cardboard milk carton

Procedure

Cut the front panel from an empty milk carton below the spout, while leaving the open spout in place. Lay the milk carton on a flat surface in a large pan. Fill the carton with sand up to the bottom of the open spout. Firmly pat down the sand. Using the sprinkler can, sprinkle water on the surface until puddles start to form. Put the brick under the back edge of the carton. Some excess water may run out the open spout.

Fill the soda bottle with water. Place the soda bottle opening at the propped edge of the milk carton. Slowly pour the full bottle of water onto the sand. You will need to have a steady, constant flow making a small stream of water. Notice the path that water takes from the back edge of the carton to the spout. Check to see where the sand that is carried by the moving water stops. Measure the depth of the eroded area of sand. Measure the width of the river.

When finished, dump the milk carton and water where an adult tells you.

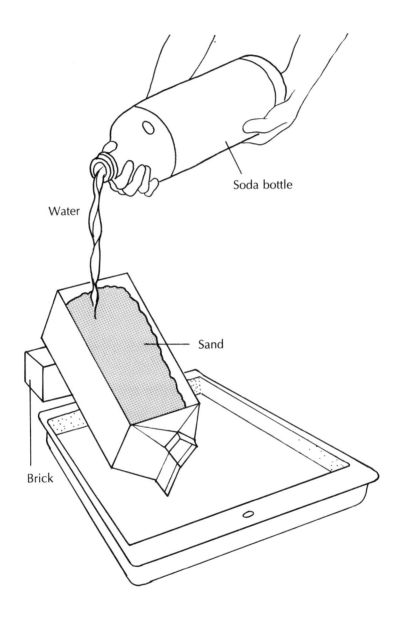

Soda bottle

Water

Sand

Brick

Observations

What does the moving water do to the sand? Where is the river the widest? Where is the eroded sand the deepest?

Discussion

Moving water is the main cause for erosion (carrying of soil from one area to another). Runoff is water that moves over the surface. Runoff usually ends up in rivers. During heavy rains, runoff carries away soil. This forms gullies (paths made by moving water). Geologists have found that if you reduce the amount and speed of water, smaller gullies will form. Small gullies join together to make bigger gullies, which allows more water to move faster. When several gullies come together we call this a river. Water flows from small rivers into bigger and then bigger rivers. A riverbed includes the moving water (river), eroded path, and surrounding area. A flood is when there is too much water to stay within the banks of the river.

Geologists have noted that the faster water is moving, the more soil it can carry. Frequently, the deepest erosion is where the most water reaches soil. Soil is carried to an area where the water slows down. When water is moving too slow, it deposits the soil particles. Moving water forms V-shaped erosion paths. Geologists can study old erosion paths. When they see a V pattern, they know it was probably caused by moving water rather than by a glacier.

Other things to try

Repeat the experiment using potting soil.

Repeat the experiment, lifting the back edge twice as high.

Repeat the experiment without a brick.

Repeat the experiment and place a very large serving spoon perpendicular to the soil, with the back surface facing the spout.

HOW DO WAVES AFFECT BEACHES?   **19**

Materials
Sand
Ruler
Two flat sponges
Measuring cup
Brick or wood block
Two baking dishes at least 9 X 13 inches (22.5 X 32.5 cm)

Procedure

Put a brick under the back edge of a baking dish. Carefully pour 4 cups (about 1 liter) of sand into the end of the baking dish opposite from the brick. This will be your beach. Remove the brick and lay the baking dish outside on a flat surface. Carefully pour water into the dish at the opposite end of the sand. Keep adding water until a depth of about 1 inch (2.5 cm) is reached at the end away from the sand. Looking through the sides of the dish, measure how deep the sand and water are at both ends. Gently place the sponge in the pan with the long side about 4 inches (10 cm) from the beach. Gently move the sponge back and forth making waves. Make five waves, and then see how the beach has changed. If there is no change, make five larger waves and observe. Repeat the procedure with a second baking dish, turning the sponge so the narrowest edge faces the beach. Gently move the sponge back and forth to make waves. Observe how the beach has changed.

When you are finished, dump the sand and water in a place recommended by an adult.

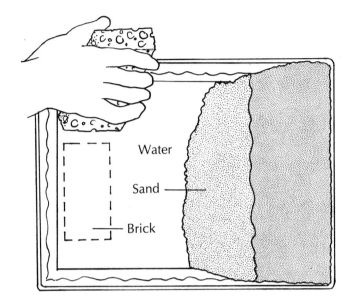

Observations

Which beach was changed more—the one with the waves made by the wide sponge or by the narrow sponge? How far away from the back edge was the sand moved? Which type of wave—the ones created by the wide sponge or by the narrow sponge—made deeper erosion?

Discussion

Moving water carries rock particles. Geologists have noticed that faster moving water carriers larger particles. As rock particles are carried, they bump into other particles, causing them to break apart into smaller pieces. Some rock particles are carried by oceans and some are carried by rivers. Geologists identify any particle that is less than 2 mm in diameter as sand.

Usually during the summer, beaches are affected little by erosion. This is because small waves are only able to carry small sand particles to the beach. But during winter, these wide sandy beaches are changed. Winter storms cause bigger waves that often carry sand away from the edge of the beach. These large waves can drastically change the shoreline. Also, the shape of a shoreline can be changed by the level of the ocean. Geologists do not recommend building on beach shorelines where there are frequent storms. There is no way to prevent beach erosion. But by understanding the ways that waves affect beaches, geologists hope to minimize harmful changes.

Other things to try

Repeat the experiment with the sponge about 1 inch (2.5 cm) from the beach.

Repeat the experiment with the sponge about 8 inches (20 cm) from the beach.

HOW DOES A DRIVEWAY AFFECT RUNOFF?

Materials

Soil
Sprinkler can
Measuring cup
Wading pool
Four wood blocks (same size) or bricks
Large rectangular cake pan with lid

Procedure

Fill a large rectangular cake pan with soil. It is best to fill it outside.

Prop one end of the cake pan lid onto two blocks inside one end of a wading pool. Measure 4 cups (about 1 liter) of water into the sprinkler can and gently pour this onto the cake pan lid. Measure the amount of water that ends up in the wading pool. Dump the water where an adult tells you. Now move the soil from the cake lid to the cake pan. Fill the pan with more soil until the pan is full. Prop up and pour the same amount of water on the cake pan as you did onto the cake lid. Measure the amount of water that drained into the wading pool.

Dump the soil and water where an adult tells you.

Observations

In which case did the greatest amount of water run into the wading pool? How did the soil affect runoff? Which one splashed the most?

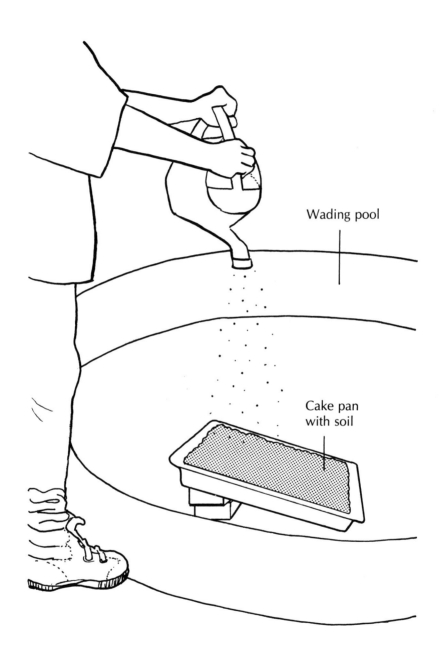

Wading pool

Cake pan
with soil

Discussion

Areas with less soil (or no soil at all) have less of a chance to hold water. Water moves quickly through these areas into streams or storm sewers which, in turn, carry the water into rivers or lakes. Geologists know that faster-moving water can carry materials such as soil. Also, the more water there is, the faster it moves. Therefore, geologists try to slow down or prevent large amounts of water from collecting in one area.

Cities with a lot of concrete roads and driveways have a greater chance for floods. Floods occur when large amounts of water fall in a short period of time. Many times, this causes water to flow onto streets and highways. Even soil areas can have floods when the soil cannot hold anymore water. Zoning commissions are concerned about the amount of roads and driveways in certain regions because they cause greater runoff.

Other things to try

Repeat the experiment, using a pan in which you have grown grass. How does the grass effect runoff?

Repeat the experiment, comparing what happens when the water is poured slowly and when it is poured rapidly.

Repeat the experiment, observing how wet soil affects the amount of runoff.

Repeat the experiment using different types of soil. Compare how sand and clay affect the amount of runoff and soil erosion.

HOW CAN YOU DETERMINE IF WATER IS HARD OR SOFT?

21

Materials

Rain	Soda bottles with screw on caps
Ruler	Liquid dish washing detergent
Tap Water	Demineralized water (available at most
Measuring cup	grocery stores)

Procedure

As water moves through rocks as groundwater, it picks up small pieces of dissolved minerals. These mineral pieces are too small to be seen, even with a hand lens. When water contains large amounts of dissolved calcium and magnesium, geologists call it hard water. Water with small amounts of dissolved calcium and magnesium is called soft water. One of the effects of using hard water is that it prevents other materials, such as soap, from dissolving in it. Hard water makes it difficult to clean things with soap and water. Hard water is not harmful to drink, but it can change its taste.

To test water to see whether it is hard or soft, put 1 cup of tap water into an empty soda bottle. Add 1 drop of dish washing detergent. Screw the cap on tight and shake it 10 times. Let it sit for one minute. Using the ruler, measure the height of soapsuds that formed. The shorter the column of soapsuds, the harder the water. Collect a cup of rainwater and repeat the test in another soda bottle. Measure the height of soapsuds. Use a cup of demineralized water and repeat the test in another soda bottle.

Observations

Which water sample was the hardest?

Which column of soapsuds was the shortest?

Discussion

The types of minerals determine whether or not they are easily removed from water. Geologists have noticed that most groundwater is fairly hard. Usually, surface water or rainwater is soft. In areas where hard water is used for washing, more soap is needed to make suds. Demineralized water is made by removing some of the minerals.

Some families want to "soften" their hard water. Commercial water softeners replace the hard forming minerals with salt. This is a chemical process. However, not all people should drink salt softened water because the salt can cause some people's blood pressure to become higher.

Other things to try

Take a sample of known hard water and boil it before testing it. How does boiling affect hardness? Check the bottom of the pan to see if mineral particles are left during boiling.

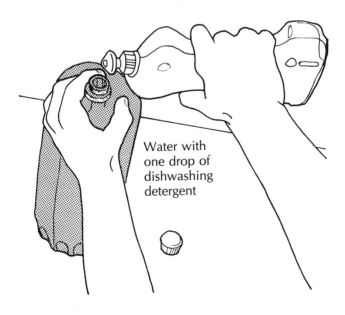

Water with one drop of dishwashing detergent

HOW DO WELLS AFFECT THE WATER TABLE?

22

Materials

Ruler	Masking tape
Straw	Marker
Cardboard	Sprinkler can
Sand	Measuring cup
Scissors	Large clear mixing bowl
Screwdriver (Phillips)	Pump from an empty spray bottle

Procedure

ASK AN ADULT TO HELP YOU WITH THIS EXPERIMENT.

Cut two pieces of cardboard into circles so that they sit about halfway down in a large mixing bowl. Tape the two pieces of cardboard together on top of one another. With a screwdriver, poke a hole through the cardboard about 2 inches (5 cm) from one edge. Cut a straw so it is about 1 inch (2.5 cm) shorter than the height of the bowl. Put the straw through the hole. The straw will become your well. Set the cardboard in the bowl. Mark on the outside of the bowl with masking tape where the bottom of the cardboard sits. Take the bowl outside and set it on a flat surface. Remove the cardboard and add water to just below the marked line. Place the cardboard back in the bowl, and tape it all the way around to the inside of the bowl. Carefully put sand on top of the cardboard until it is 4 inches (10 cm) thick. Put the pipe from the pump of an empty bottle into the straw. While holding the straw in place point the pump away from the bowl. Now pump until no water comes out. Looking through the side of the bowl, check to see if water is still there.

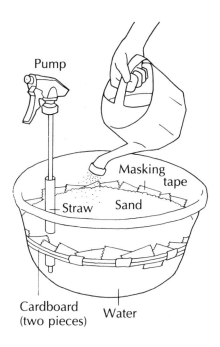

Pump

Masking
tape

Straw   Sand

Cardboard
(two pieces)   Water

Measure 1 cup (about 250 ml) of water and, using the sprinkler can, gently pour this amount on the sand. Check how long it takes the water to get below the cardboard. Check to see if you can now pump water again.

When finished, dump the materials where an adult tells you to and rinse the bowl.

Observations

What happened when the water started to get low in the bowl? When was it the easiest to get water from the well? How long did it take for water to move through the cardboard?

Discussion

Water that is found below the surface of the earth is called ground-water. Geologists are interested in where groundwater can be found. Frequently, groundwater can only be found very deep under-ground. Wells must be dug into the layer where the groundwater is found. Usually these wells are pipes less than 3 inches (7.5 cm) across that are sunk into the earth. The straw in the experiment represented the pipe from a well. Usually, the bottom of the pipe is covered with a heavy screen which prevents material other than water from getting into the pipe.

The top of the layer of underground water is called the <u>water table</u>. Groundwater can be in rocks, such as sandstone, or between layers of rock. The layer below the water table has to be able to prevent water from passing through it. Otherwise, the groundwater would keep going deeper into the ground and we would need to continuously dig deeper wells. There are places where the water table is at the surface. Geologists call these places <u>springs</u>. These areas are usually found in low lying areas as compared to the tops of hills or mountains.

As rain falls, water slowly moves through the layers of soil and rock until it reaches the water table. If there has been a drought and people use a lot of groundwater, a well can run dry. It takes a very long time for rainwater to reach the water table.

Geologists must test groundwater to determine whether it is safe for human use. If a water supply is of poor quality, they need to dig deeper to a lower water table.

Other things to try

Repeat the experiment using two pumping wells. How long does it take until the water no longer can be pumped.

Prop the edge of the bowl which is near the well on top of a book. How can the well be dry when there is still water present?

Sprinkle some dry powdered drink mix on the top of the sand. Then, sprinkle 1 cup (about 250 ml) of water on the sand. How long does it take until water from the well becomes colored.

HOW DOES POLLUTION INFLUENCE **23** DRINKING WATER?

Materials

Ruler	Marker
Straw	Sprinkler can
Cardboard	Measuring cup
Sand	Blue food coloring
Scissors	Large clear mixing bowl
Screwdriver	Pump from an empty spray bottle
Masking tape	

Procedure

ASK AN ADULT TO HELP YOU WITH THIS EXPERIMENT.

Cut two pieces of cardboard into circles so that they sit about halfway down in a large mixing bowl. Tape the two pieces of cardboard together on top of one another. With a screwdriver, poke a hole through the cardboard about 2 inches (5 cm) from one edge. Cut a straw so it is about 1 inch (2.5 cm) shorter than the height of the bowl. Put the straw through the hole. The straw will become your well. Set the cardboard in the bowl. Mark on the outside of the bowl with masking tape where the bottom of the cardboard sits. Take the bowl outside and set it on a flat surface. Remove the cardboard and add water to just below the marked line. Add five drops of blue food coloring to the water. Place the cardboard back in the bowl, and tape it all the way around to the inside of the bowl. Carefully put sand on top of the cardboard until it is 4 inches (10 cm) thick. Put the pipe from the pump of an empty bottle into the straw. While holding the straw in place point the pump away from the bowl. Now pump until no water comes out. Looking through the side of the bowl, check to see if water is still there.

Measure 1 cup (about 250 ml) of water and, using the sprinkler can, gently pour this amount on the sand. Check how long it takes the water to get below the cardboard. Check to see if you can now pump water again.

Again, gently sprinkle 1 cup (about 250 ml) of water onto the sand. Pump out the water. Keep adding water then pumping until the water is almost clear.

When finished, dump materials where an adult tells you to and rinse the bowl.

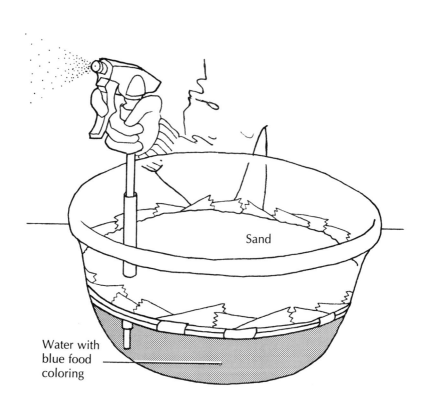

Sand

Water with
blue food
coloring

Observations

How much water does it take for the well water to become clear?

Discussion

The blue food coloring is a <u>pollutant</u> (contaminant or unwanted substance) in the groundwater. Geologists frequently test the groundwater in wells to make sure it is not polluted. Many pollutants are clear, so many tests other than appearance must be done. Groundwater flows from one area to another. So, when geologists find one polluted well, they notify others who are using that source of groundwater. Often, geologists are able to find the cause of the pollution. Then they try to remove it. Sometimes this requires digging up and cleaning certain areas, an expensive way to remove pollution.

In earlier times, people threw their trash onto the ground, especially into ditches. As metal parts in the garbage rusted, tiny rust particles were carried with surface water into the groundwater. Some of today's polluted groundwater is due to this disposal system of previous generations. Geologists must frequently find new ways of handling particular wastes. They are concerned with both our current and future pollution problems.

Other things to try

Bury some powdered drink mix at one spot in the sand in the above experiment. As you sprinkle water over the sand, notice how the coloring spreads.

Repeat the experiment with water containing 2 drops of green food coloring. What color is the water from the well?

WHAT HAPPENS WHEN PLATE BOUNDARIES MOVE?

24

Materials
Ruler
Wax paper
Cake frosting
Graham crackers
Hard-boiled egg
Table knife

Procedure

Take a cooled hard-boiled egg with the shell still on and drop it three times on a counter or table from a height of 6 inches (15 cm). Notice the cracks that form and how the shell still holds the inside of the egg in place. This is similar to the earth. The earth is composed of a series of plates, like the cracked shell, that are slowly moving. These plates float on the material below. Even the ground under the oceans has plates that are floating. Carefully examine the cracked shell. You will notice some places where a piece of shell is under another piece, and some places where one piece has slid against another piece. The earth's plates have the same arrangement.

Place a sheet of wax paper on a flat surface. With a table knife, spread a thick layer of cake frosting the size of an envelope on the wax paper. Lay two graham cracker pieces that are about the same size gently on the frosting. There should be about 1/2 inch (1 cm) space between the crackers. The layer of frosting should be larger than the two crackers. To demonstrate plates moving apart, gently press down and slowly push the two graham crackers apart.

Observations

On the egg, how many places were there where the shell slid under another piece of shell? How may places had no shell? In how many places did pieces of shell slide past other pieces? What happened to the frosting when you pushed the crackers apart?

Discussion

Geologists believe that there are less than twenty plates on the earth. They have also noticed that the edges of the plates are the places where earthquakes and volcanoes occur. Earthquakes occur where there is a large movement of plates.

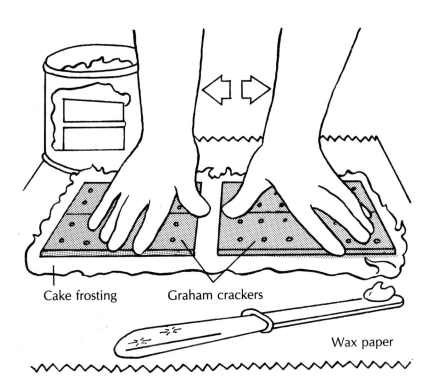

Cake frosting   Graham crackers

Wax paper

The plates move very slowly, so slowly in fact that we cannot tell they are moving. The plates are always moving in one of three ways—colliding with each other, spreading apart, or sliding past one another. Geologists are not certain about what causes the plates to move. Many currently think that deep within the earth there are areas of heat that cause the movement of the plates.

Your graham crackers represent what geologists believe happens at the mid-Atlantic ridge. This is an edge of two plates that run north to south that are slowly moving apart. As you moved the graham crackers apart, the frosting came up. At the mid-Atlantic ridge new rocks are formed. To make room for these moving plates, other plate edges are sliding past and colliding with other plates. The widening of the mid-Atlantic ridge is slowly making the Atlantic Ocean larger.

Other things to try

Locate the mid-Atlantic ridge on a world map.

Locate regions of earthquakes on a world map.

Locate regions of volcanoes.

WHAT HAPPENS WHEN TWO PLATES COLLIDE?

25

Materials
Cup

Graham crackers

Knife

Cassette tape plastic case (empty)

Procedure
Cut a graham cracker to be the same size as a cassette tape. Lay a plastic cassette case and graham cracker end to end on a flat surface. Gently push the two together and notice how one slides under the other.

Put about 1 inch (2.5 cm) of water in a cup large enough for the graham cracker to stand in. Quickly dip the ends of 2 crackers into the water. Place the wet ends of the crackers almost touching each other. From the dry ends, gently push the 2 crackers until it becomes difficult to push. Let the crackers dry.

Observations
Which ended up on top—the graham cracker or the cassette case? What happened when the wet ends of the crackers were pushed together?

Discussion
Geologists have noticed that when oceanic plates and continental plates come together, the oceanic plate (graham cracker) slides under the continental plate (cassette case). This results in everything buried on the edge of the oceanic plate being pushed deeper as the plates continue to move. This build-up of movement causes earthquakes, such as the famous 1906 and 1989 San Francisco earthquakes.

Sometimes two continental plates are moving in opposite directions and slide into each other. The wet ends of the graham crackers represent what geologists think has caused the formation of the Himalayan Mountains. The continental plate of India is moving into the continental plate of Asia, causing a bulge.

Other things to try

Locate on a map or a globe the San Andreas fault where the San Francisco earthquakes have occurred. Using the fingers on both of your hands, show how an oceanic plate is sliding under a continental plate.

Locate the Himalayan Mountains on a map. How tall is the highest peak, Mt. Everest?

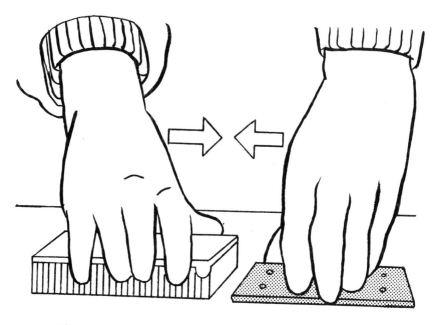

Plastic cassette case

Graham cracker

WHAT HAPPENS WHEN A GLACIER MELTS?

26

Materials

Wading pool	Potting soil
Gravel	Half-gallon cardboard milk carton
Ruler	Bricks
Sand	Board
Scissors	Masking tape

Procedure

Cut off the top of an empty milk carton. Put two handfuls each of gravel, potting soil, and sand into the carton. Add water to a depth of about 6 inches (15 cm). Stir the sand, potting soil, gravel, and water. Then place the carton in the freezer until the next day. When frozen, this will be your glacier.

Outside, prop one end of the wading pool with bricks or boards to a height of about 1 inch (2.5 cm). Remove the glacier from the freezer and cut away the carton. Place the glacier at the highest end of the wading pool. Tape a board to the wading pool and the glacier to hold the glacier in place. You will now need to wait for the entire glacier to melt. You can check it every 15 minutes to see what is happening to the gravel, potting soil and sand as the glacier melts. After the glacier has completely melted, measure the distance the gravel, sand, and potting soil were carried from the melted glacier.

Dump the contents of the wading pool in a place recommended by an adult.

Observations

Which was carried the farthest from the glacier—gravel, sand, or potting soil? What happened to the gravel that was on the sides of the glacier? Were materials located at the front of the glacier carried farther?

Discussion

Geologists have measured the movement of the materials inside glaciers and have found that they move fastest at the center and slowest at the edges. However, this movement is fairly slow (i.e., a few inches per day). When glaciers melt they are called receding,

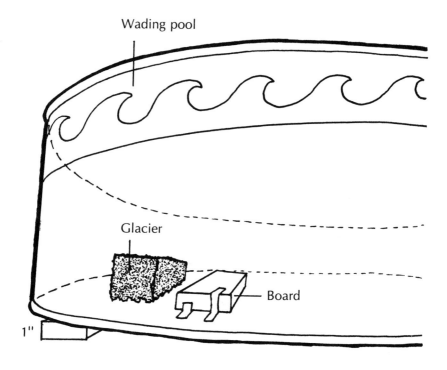

Wading pool

Glacier

Board

1"

leaving behind the pieces of rock that they picked up. As more ice melts, the pieces of sand, potting soil, and gravel are carried away from the glacier.

The biggest pieces of gravel are usually left near the glacier because it takes a lot of water to transport the gravel. A slowly melting glacier releases only a small amount of water. Therefore, the smallest particles are carried the farthest because they need the least moving water to carry them.

Other things to try

Repeat the experiment using a glacier made of different types of materials. Compare the melting of a sand glacier to the melting of a gravel glacier.

Repeat the experiment, and shine a light on the glacier to speed up its melting. Compare the travel distances for sand and gravel.

HOW DOES WATER AFFECT SANDSTONE?

27

Materials

Scale (diet food)
Two wide-mouthed jars
Pieces of sandstone (available from a rock shop)

Procedure

Place the scale on a flat surface. Have an adult help you adjust it. The scale will record weight, usually in grams. To get an idea of how much a gram (g) is, a nickel weighs about 5 g. Grams are a small unit of weight. Your scale will probably only measure objects that weigh less than 300 g. To weigh an object, carefully place it on the scale. If the object is too heavy, the scale will stop at the highest number. If this happens, quickly remove the object to prevent it from stretching the spring on the scale. If the spring is stretched too much, the scale will not record accurately. Practice weighing objects such as pencils, spoons, and watches.

Take two small pieces of sandstone that are about the same size. They must be able to fit into the jars. Weigh each separately on the scale. If they are too heavy, find smaller pieces. Record the weight of each for comparison. Pour 1 cup (250 ml) of water into each jar. Place a piece of sandstone in each jar. Carefully screw on the lids. Lay one of the jars with the sandstone on its side. Leave the other jar standing upright. Leave the sandstone in the water overnight. The next day, remove the pieces of sandstone. Weigh each separately and record their weights. Set the same pieces of sandstone in two empty jars, in the same positions that you placed them in the water. Replace the lids

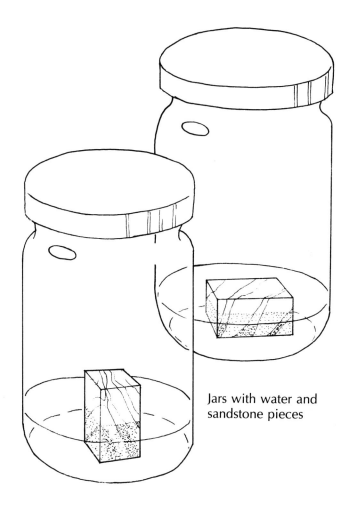

Jars with water and
sandstone pieces

and leave them overnight. One will be on its side, the other standing
upright. Check the jars the next day.

Dump the water in a place recommended by an adult.

Observations

How much did the sandstone pieces weigh when they were dry?
How much did they weigh after sitting in water? Which gained the most

weight—the piece laying flat or the piece standing up in the water? What caused the change in weight? What did you notice in the sealed jars on the last day?

Discussion

Sandstone has air spaces between each piece of sand. When comparing sandstone to other rocks, geologists consider sandstone to have a large amount of air space because the pieces of sand do not fit together tightly. When the sandstone was placed in water, its air spaces were filled with water. The movement of the water into the sandstone is slow. For the piece standing in the water, the water can be higher than the top of the sandstone. This is just how straws work. For a smaller straw, the water sticks closer together and air forces water up higher in the straw.

The extra weight in your pieces of sandstone is due to the water. Groundwater moves through sandstone in a similar way. When you placed the wet sandstone into empty jars, some of the water moved out of the sandstone. Geologists have noted that water generally moves from an area of greater amount to an area of lesser amount. They say that it is trying to "find an equal level."

Geologists have also noted that even tightly packed rocks still have some air spaces. Water can fill these air spaces. But when it takes a long time to move water through rocks, as with limestone, they are a poor source of groundwater because the water is used much faster than it could be replaced.

Other things to try

Repeat the experiment with various amounts of water.

Repeat the experiment using an igneous rock such as granite.

WHAT IS A GEOLOGIC TIME SCALE? 28

Materials
Adding machine tape (at least 5 meters long)
Metric ruler (use the metric units of a regular ruler)

Procedure

This experiment uses only metric measurements to make it easier to understand the geologic time scale. To geologists, the geologic time scale is everything that has happened since the earth was formed (over 4.5 billion years ago). You will be representing time where 1 mm equals 1,000,000 years. When finished you will have a time line of major geological history. Reminder: 10 mm = 1 cm and 100 cm = 1 m.

Unroll about 5 m of adding machine tape. Measure 10 cm from the right end of the tape. Draw a line across the tape and label it "present." Measure 1 mm left from present and draw a line across the tape. Label this "Ice Age begins." Measure 1 mm left from the Ice Age and draw a line across the tape. Label this "When Humans First Appeared." Measure another 63 mm (6.3 cm) left and draw a line across the tape and label it "Dinosaurs Disappear." Measure another 100 mm (10 cm) left and draw a line across the tape, labelling it "When Birds First Appeared." Measure another 100 mm (10 cm) to the left and draw a line across the tape, and label it "Dinosaurs Are Major Land Animal." Measure 10 mm left again and draw a line across the tape, and label it "First Mammal-like Animals Appear." Now measure 75 mm (7.5 cm) to the left and draw a line across the tape. Label this line "First Reptiles Appear." Another 85 mm (8.5 cm) to the left, draw a line across the tape and label it "First Amphibians Appear." Measure 45 mm (4.5 cm) to the left and label this line "First Animals Appear" (Scorpion-like animal). Measure another 85 mm (8.5 cm) to the left and draw a line across the tape, labelling it "First Fish Appear" (first animal with backbone). Draw another line 80 mm (8 cm) to the left and label this line "First Animals With Shells Appear." Measure another 120 mm (12 cm) to the left. Draw a line across the tape and label it "First Life Appears" (bacteria). Finally, measure an additional 1,000 millimeters (100 cm or 1 m) to the left. Draw the last line and label it "Earth Was Formed."

Observations

How much longer have fish been on the earth than birds? How long after dinosaurs disappeared did humans appear? How does the animal life on earth compare with the age of the earth?

Discussion

The geologic time scale allows geologists to arrange in sequence events that have happened. In your tape, 1 mm = 1 million years (1 m = 1 billion years!). Frequently, geologists report time in millions of years ago. They are not able to establish the exact date. Therefore, their time line represents one event in relation to another event. Geologists refer to events when certain living creatures first appeared or disappeared. For example, the age of dinosaurs was about 120 million years long (on your time line, 120 mm).

Geologists have studied evidence of past life over the entire earth by examining fossils. The geologic time scale does not have all the fossils in one place. Therefore, it has been difficult for geologists to piece together the earth's history. Particular layers of rock with their fossils are identified as either older or younger than another area. This requires the careful study of several regions to make sure that geologists are correct.

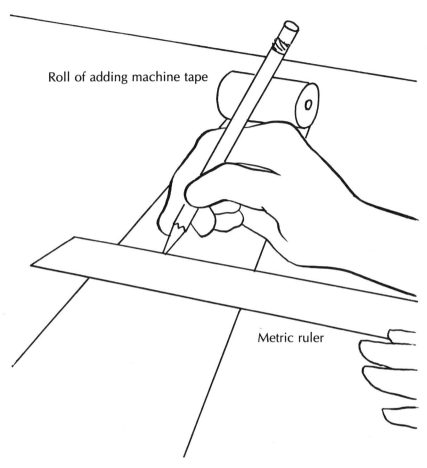

Roll of adding machine tape

Metric ruler

Other things to try

Label the following events on your tape:

"First Plants Appear"—410 million years before present;

"Age of Dinosaurs"—65-245 million years before present;

"Age of Mammals"—begins 65 million years ago.

WHAT SOIL DO EARTHWORMS PREFER?

29

Materials

Moist soil	Pencil
Moist sand	Tape
Black garbage bag	Scissors
Rubber bands	Large mayonnaise jar
Earthworms	Black construction paper
Dead leaves	

Procedure

Put about 2 inches (5 cm) of moist soil in the bottom of a mayonnaise jar. Add about 2 inches (5 cm) of moist sand on top. Next, put about the same amount of moist soil in the jar. Continue alternating layers of moist sand and soil until the jar is almost full. Place 5 earthworms and several dead leaves on top of the final layer. Cut a piece of a black garbage bag so that it will cover the opening of the jar. Use the rubber band to hold the piece of garbage bag around the top of the jar. Gently poke small air holes in the garbage bag lid with the pencil. Tape a piece of black construction paper around the jar so that the earthworms will be in the dark.

Let the jar stand for one week. Without tipping the jar, remove the construction paper.

After making your observations, dump the soil and earthworms outside where an adult tells you.

Observations

Where are the earthworms in the jar? What happened to the leaves? Are the burrows (earthworm tunnels) straight or angled? Are all the burrows the same width? Are there still layers of sand and soil?

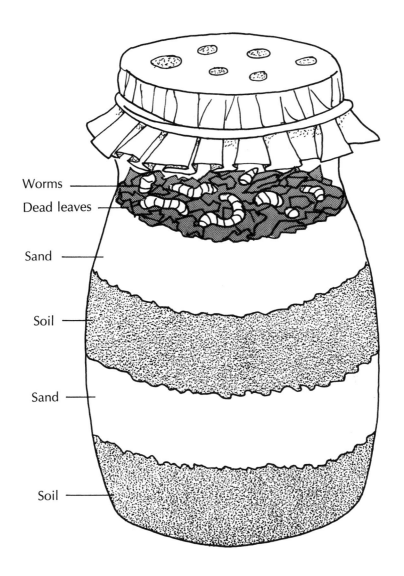

Worms

Dead leaves

Sand

Soil

Sand

Soil

Discussion

Earthworms stay in their burrows during the day. At night, sometimes, they will crawl on the surface. Earthworms like to eat leaves. Frequently, they pull the leaves into their burrows. As they burrow, earthworms swallow some of the soil. Also, they eat pieces of rotting plants and small dead animals in the soil. As they burrow, they mix up layers of soil.

Geologists have noted that earthworms improve our soil. They eat dead plants. Their wastes are added to the soil making it better for plants to grow. In addition, their burrows make air spaces, which make it easier for plants to grow. These air spaces provide oxygen for plants and animals that live in the soil to breathe. These burrows also allow rain water to drain away.

Other things to try

Repeat the experiment, using different types of dead leaves (grass, lettuce, cabbage, carrots, etc.) to see which earthworms prefer.

Using a plastic shoe box, prepare the layers of soil and sand as you did with the jar. Wrap the outside with black construction paper. Cover only half of the top with a black cover. Check the following day to see where the burrows are found.

In a cake pan, put two small paper towels in the bottom, leaving about 2 inches (5 cm) between them. Now wet one towel. Place three earthworms in the space between the towels. Check one hour later to see where the earthworms have moved.

In a dark plastic shoe box, put a damp paper towel on the bottom. Put a few earthworms in the center of the box. Cover half of the box with a piece of cardboard. Check one hour later to see where the earthworms have moved.

30

WHAT PREVENTS A BALANCED ROCK FROM FALLING?

Materials

Cork
Paring knife
Rounded toothpick
Two sharpened pencils of equal length

Procedure

Frequently, we may see large pointed rocks loosely sitting on flat surfaces. It appears that strong winds could blow them over. However, these balanced rocks have been in this position for many years. This experiment will allow you to figure out what keeps them balanced.

Stand a cork upright. Stick the points of two sharpened pencils on opposite sides of the cork. Set the bottom of the cork on the tip of one of your fingers. If it does not balance, adjust the pencils until you can balance the cork on your finger.

Remove the cork (with pencils) from your finger and turn it upside down. Ask an adult to help you carefully cut a toothpick in half with a knife. While holding the cork in place, force the pointed end of one half of the toothpick through the center of the cork, perpendicular to the pencils, until only about a centimeter is protruding. Ask an adult to help you use the knife to shape the end of the toothpick into a point. Now, stand the point of the sharpened toothpick on your finger. If it falls over, adjust the pencils until it does balance.

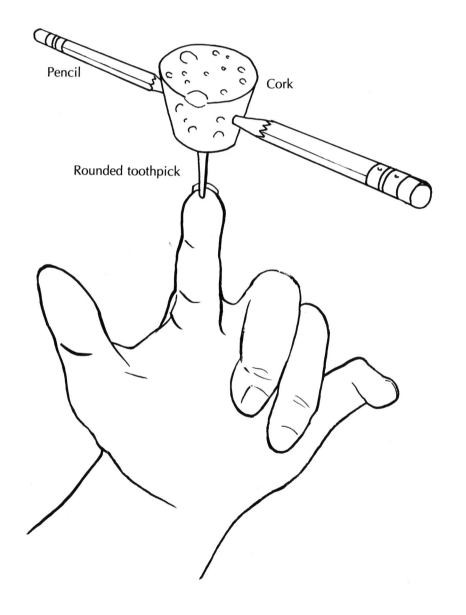

Pencil

Cork

Rounded toothpick

Observations

What happens when you stand the cork on the point of your finger?

What happens when you stand it on the side of your finger?

Discussion

Gravity is a force that attracts all objects towards the center of the earth. The place on all objects where all the weight is centered is called the center of gravity. Once the weight is no longer over the center of gravity, an object falls over. Geologists have determined that rocks with a high center of gravity are rarely balanced. The reason that balanced rocks are still standing is because they have a low center of gravity.

Humans also have a center of gravity. Each time we take a step, our center of gravity moves forward. If it did not, we would fall down each time we moved. Your center of gravity is someplace between your hips and chest. We are able to balance ourselves without thinking. Have a friend stand up, then lift one leg and stretch it out as far as possible. Notice how your friend leans over or lifts an arm to keep balanced. Women in the last few months of pregnancy have difficulty getting up from chairs because their centers of gravity have shifted.

Other things to try

Repeat the experiment using three pencils stuck in the side of the cork.

Repeat the experiment using only one pencil that is stuck in the side of the cork.

Repeat the experiment using a long toothpick or wood skewer rather than half of a toothpick.

Where to Get Science Supplies

The following companies sell mineral samples and other science supplies. To order materials for your experiments, write or telephone the nearest company to find out about prices. Then send your order to the company with a check or money order to cover the cost. You can also ask your teacher to order materials for you on school stationery.

Carolina Biological Supply
    2700 York Road
    Burlington, NC 27215
    (919) 584-0381

Edmund Scientific Company
    101 East Glouchester Pike
    Barrington, NJ 08007-1380
    (609) 573-6250

Fisher Scientific
    4901 W. Le Moyne Street
    Chicago, IL 60651
    (800) 621-4769

Frey Scientific Company
    905 Hickory Lane
    P.O. Box 8101
    Mansfield, OH 44905
    (800) 225-FREY

Sargent-Welch
    7400 North Linder Avenue
    P.O. Box 1026
    Skokie, IL 60077
    (800) 727-4368

Science Kit and Boreal
    Laboratories
    777 East Park Drive
    Tonawanda, NY 14150-6782
    (800) 828-7777
    —OR—

Science Kit and Boreal
    Laboratories
    P.O. Box 2726
    Sante Fe Springs, CA
    90670-4490

Ward's Natural Science
    Establishment, Inc.
    5100 West Henrietta Road
    P.O. Box 92912
    Rochester, NY 14692
    (800) 962-2660

COMPLETE LIST OF MATERIALS
USED IN EXPERIMENTS

Aluminum pie tin

Baking dishes (9 x 13 inches)
balloon, large
BBs
bowl, large clear mixing
bricks or wood blocks
bucket

Cake frosting
cake pan, rectangular with lid
cardboard, corrugated
case, plastic cassette tape
clay
clay, modeling
coal*
construction paper, black
cork, wine bottle

Demineralized water
detergent, liquid dish washing
dinner plate, 10-inch
dowel rod
dropper, medicine

Earthworms
egg, hard-boiled

Ferrous sulfate iron tablets
food coloring, blue & yellow
fork (meat)

Garbage bag, black
glasses, clear
graham crackers
gravel*

Gummi Bears™

Hammer
hand lens or magnifying glass

Jars, clear plastic (with lids)
jars, wide-mouthed (with lids)
juice cans, 46-ounce

Knife, paring & table

Leaves, dead
lid to 18-ounce jelly jar

Magnet
magnifying glass or hand lens
masking tape
measuring cup
measuring spoons
milk cartons, quart size & 1/2 gallon
mustard seed

Needles
newspaper
nylon stockings, old

Pans, large shallow
paper, white
paring knife
pencils
pen, marking
powdered alum (a spice)
pump, empty spray bottle

Rocks, small*
rubber bands

rulers, metric & English

Salt
sand, fine*
sandstone pieces*
sauce pan
scale, diet food
scissors, kitchen
screwdriver, Phillips
sheetrock (or smooth board)
shoe box
soda bottle, 2-liter with screw cap
soil, potting
soil, samples of
sponges, flat
sprinkler can
straw, plastic
styrofoam cups
subsoil

Tablespoon
tape, 5 meters of adding machine
teaspoon
tomato paste can, small
toothpick, rounded
topsoil
trowel

Wading pool
washcloths, old
water, rain
water, tap
wax paper
wood blocks or bricks
wood larger than piece of coal

* available from a rock shop

Index